ONE-POT

Simple recipes for hearty, slow-cooked meals

CONTENTS

Guide to symbols

The recipes in this book are accompanied by symbols that alert you to important information.

 Tells you how many people the recipe serves, or how much is produced.

 Indicates how much time you will need to prepare and cook a dish. Next to this symbol you will also find out if additional time is required for such things as marinating, standing, proving, or cooling. You need to read the recipe to find out exactly how much extra time is needed.

 Alerts you to what has to be done before you can begin to cook the recipe, or to parts of the recipe that take a long time to complete.

 Denotes that special equipment is required. Where possible, alternatives are given.

 Accompanies freezing information.

3

Quick fish stew

This stew can be made even more quickly if you use cooked prawns instead of fresh ones.

INGREDIENTS

1 tbsp olive oil
1 onion, finely chopped
3 garlic cloves, grated or finely chopped
5 celery sticks, chopped
2 carrots, chopped
salt
sprig of thyme, leaves only
1 tsp tomato purée
1 glass of dry white wine

4 tomatoes, skinned
900ml (1½ pints) light fish stock
2 haddock fillets, about 675g (1½lb) total weight, cut into chunky pieces
200g (7 oz) raw prawns, peeled and deveined
handful of flat-leaf parsley, finely chopped

METHOD

1 Heat the oil in a pan over a low heat, and add the onion, garlic, celery, and carrots, along with a pinch of salt and the thyme. Sweat gently for about 10 minutes.

2 Now stir in the tomato purée, increase the heat to high, and add the wine. Let it simmer for a couple of minutes, then add the tomatoes (squashing them with a fork) and a little of the stock, and simmer a little more. Pour in almost all of the remaining stock, and bring to the boil. Reduce the heat slightly, and simmer for 10 minutes. At this point, you can blend the sauce with a hand-held blender until smooth, if you like. Top up with the remaining stock if needed.

3 Add the fish and prawns, cover the pan, and cook for 5–10 minutes until the fish is cooked through. Serve hot with fresh, crusty bread.

serves 4

prep 10 mins
• cook 30 mins

blender

Prawn makhani

This creamy, spicy recipe is based on a classic curry from North India.

INGREDIENTS

700g (1lb 9 oz) (shelled weight) uncooked prawns, peeled and deveined
salt and freshly ground black pepper
6 garlic cloves, grated or finely chopped
15cm (6in) piece of fresh root ginger, peeled and grated, or finely chopped
3 tbsp vegetable oil
200ml (7fl oz) thick natural yogurt
2–3 tsp chilli powder

2 cinnamon sticks, broken into pieces
4 red chillies, deseeded and finely chopped
6 cardamom pods, crushed
700g (1lb 9 oz) tomatoes
125g (4½ oz) cashew nuts, ground, plus a handful, roughly chopped, to garnish
2–3 tsp ground fenugreek
200ml (7fl oz) double cream

METHOD

1 Season the prawns with salt and pepper and toss with half the garlic, half the ginger, 1 teaspoon of the oil, the yogurt, and chilli powder. Heat a large deep-sided frying pan, then add the prawns with as much of the yogurt coating as you can, and cook over a high heat, tossing them all the time, for 5–8 minutes, or until no longer pink. Remove and set aside.

2 Heat the remaining oil in the pan, add the rest of the ginger and garlic, the cinnamon, chillies, and cardamom pods, and cook over a low heat, stirring occasionally, for 2 minutes. Add the tomatoes and cook for 10 minutes, or until they start to reduce. Cover with a little hot water and simmer for a further 10 minutes, or until puréed.

3 Push the tomato mixture through a sieve into a food processor and whiz until smooth. Return to the pan, then stir through the ground cashew nuts and fenugreek and simmer for 10 minutes, adding a little hot water if the sauce starts to look too thick. Add the prawns along with the cream, stir, taste, and season, if needed. Cook for 5 minutes, then garnish with the chopped cashew nuts and serve with rice.

serves 8

prep 20 mins
• cook 40 mins

food processor

Smoked fish and anchovy gratin

A creamy and flavourful fish dish with a crisp, golden topping.

INGREDIENTS

125g (4½ oz) smoked
   mackerel
125g (4½ oz) smoked salmon
8–12 whole anchovies in
   oil, drained
4 waxy potatoes, peeled,
   boiled, and sliced
knob of butter, melted

For the sauce
knob of butter
1 onion, finely chopped
1 garlic clove, grated or finely chopped
1 tbsp plain flour
300ml (10fl oz) milk
salt and freshly ground black pepper
handful of curly-leaf parsley, finely chopped

METHOD

1 Preheat the oven to 200°C (400°F/Gas 6). To make the sauce, melt the butter in a pan over a low heat. Add the onion, and sweat gently for about 5 minutes until soft and translucent, then add the garlic and cook for a few seconds more. Remove from the heat, and stir through the flour using a wooden spoon, then add a little milk and beat until smooth.

2 Return the pan to the heat, and slowly add the rest of the milk, stirring until the sauce has thickened. Season well with salt and pepper, and stir through the parsley.

3 Layer the smoked fish and anchovies in an ovenproof dish, then spoon over the sauce and gently combine. Top with a layer of potatoes, brush with melted butter, and bake in the oven for 15–20 minutes until golden, crispy, and heated through. Serve with a crisp green salad.

serves 4

prep 10 mins
• cook 30 mins

Smoked haddock with spinach and pancetta

This deliciously satisfying dish is great for a quick supper.

INGREDIENTS

15g (½ oz) butter, plus extra for greasing

1 tbsp olive oil

1 onion, finely chopped

100g (3½ oz) pancetta or bacon, chopped

450g (1lb) spinach

100g (3½ oz) crème fraîche

salt and freshly ground black pepper

75g (2½ oz) Parmesan cheese, grated

800g (1¾ lb) smoked fillets of haddock or cod, skinned

juice of ½ lemon

30g (1 oz) fresh breadcrumbs

METHOD

1 Preheat the oven to 190°C (375°F/Gas 5) and grease an ovenproof serving dish with butter. Melt the oil and butter together in a frying pan and fry the onion and pancetta or bacon for 5 minutes.

2 Add the spinach and stir until wilted, then stir in the crème fraîche, seasoning, and three-quarters of the Parmesan. Simmer until slightly thickened.

3 Spoon the spinach mixture into the ovenproof dish and place the fish on top. Sprinkle with the lemon juice. Scatter with breadcrumbs and the remaining Parmesan, and bake for 15–20 minutes, or until the fish is cooked through and flakes easily.

serves 6

prep 10 mins
• cook 15–20 mins

Courgette, herb, and lemon tagine

A tasty vegetarian version of the famous Moroccan speciality.

INGREDIENTS

2 tbsp olive oil

2 red onions, finely chopped

salt and freshly ground black pepper

4 garlic cloves, grated or finely chopped

pinch of fennel seeds

pinch of ground cinnamon

2–3 tsp harissa (depending on taste),
   plus extra, to serve

4 preserved lemons, halved, pith
   removed, and halved again

2 x 400g cans whole tomatoes, chopped

1 head of broccoli, broken into florets

6 courgettes, sliced

juice of 1 lemon

handful of dill, finely chopped

400g (14 oz) couscous

handful of flat-leaf parsley, finely
   chopped

lemon wedges, to serve

METHOD

1 Heat half the oil in a large heavy-based pan, add the onions, and cook over a low heat for 8 minutes, or until soft and translucent. Season well with salt and pepper. Stir through the garlic, fennel seeds, cinnamon, harissa, and preserved lemons.

2 Add the tomatoes and stir well, crushing them with the back of a wooden spoon. Bring to the boil, then reduce to a simmer and cook over a low heat for 30–40 minutes. If the sauce starts to dry out, top up with a little hot water.

3 Cook the broccoli in a pan of boiling salted water for 3–5 minutes or until tender, then drain and refresh in cold water. Drain again and put to one side. Heat the remaining oil in another frying pan, add the courgettes, and season with salt and pepper. Cook over a low heat, stirring frequently, for 5 minutes, or until they start to colour a little. Add the lemon juice and stir the dill through.

4 Meanwhile, put the couscous in a large bowl and pour over just enough boiling water to cover it. Leave for 10 minutes, then fluff up with a fork and season well with salt and pepper. Add the broccoli and courgettes to the sauce and stir through the parsley. Serve with the couscous, lemon wedges, and a spoonful of harissa.

serves 8

**prep 25 mins
• cook 1 hr**

Vegetarian leek and mushroom lasagne

Grated mushrooms add a meaty texture and chillies a pleasant heat to this dish.

INGREDIENTS

6 tbsp olive oil

4 large leeks, cut into 5mm (¼in) slices

550g (1¼lb) chestnut mushrooms, sliced

250g (9 oz) chestnut mushrooms, grated

2–3 red chillies, deseeded and finely chopped

6 garlic cloves, chopped

150ml (5fl oz) dry white wine

small handful of thyme leaves

2 tbsp plain flour

900ml (1½ pints) milk

350g (12 oz) Cheddar cheese, grated

6 tomatoes, roughly chopped, plus 1 extra, sliced

salt and freshly ground black pepper

450g (1lb) lasagne sheets

METHOD

1 Pre-heat the oven to 180°C (350°F/Gas 4). Heat the oil in a large heavy-based pan, add the leeks, and cook over a low heat, stirring frequently, for 5 minutes, or until starting to soften. Stir in the mushrooms and cook, stirring frequently, for 5 minutes, or until they release their juices. Add the chillies and garlic, and cook for 1 minute. Pour in the wine, raise the heat, and boil for 3 minutes while the alcohol evaporates.

2 Stir in the thyme, then add the flour and mix well. Add a little of the milk, mix well, then add the rest of the milk and cook for 5 minutes, stirring frequently. Add almost all the cheese (reserve some for the topping), remove from the heat, and combine well. Add the chopped tomatoes and season well with salt and pepper.

3 Put a 1cm (½in) layer of the mixture in the bottom of a large ovenproof dish, then cover evenly with a layer of the lasagne sheets. Pour in another layer of sauce and cover with lasagne. Repeat the process until all the sauce is used up – you need to finish with a layer of sauce. Top with the remaining cheese and the sliced tomato.

4 Place the dish in the oven for 30 minutes, or until browning on top and piping hot.

serves 8

prep 25 mins
• cook 20 mins

freeze, uncooked in its dish, for up to 3 months; cook straight from frozen for 30–40 mins to serve

Chicken casserole with herb dumplings

Serve this hearty winter dish with freshly steamed greens.

INGREDIENTS

1 tbsp plain flour
salt and freshly ground black pepper
8 chicken thighs and drumsticks
2 tbsp olive oil
2 carrots, sliced
2 leeks, sliced
2 celery sticks, sliced
½ swede, diced
500ml (16fl oz) chicken stock
2 tbsp Worcestershire sauce

For the dumplings

125g (4½ oz) self-raising flour
60g (2 oz) light suet, shredded
1 tbsp flat-leaf parsley, chopped
1 tsp dried mixed herbs
salt and freshly ground black pepper

METHOD

1 Season the flour with salt and pepper. Toss the chicken pieces in the flour to coat. Heat half the oil in the casserole and fry the chicken, turning often, for 6 minutes, or until brown all over. Remove and keep warm. Pour the fat from the casserole.

2 Add the remaining oil, carrots, leeks, celery, and swede to the casserole, and stir over the heat for 3–4 minutes to colour lightly. Return the chicken to the casserole, and add the stock and Worcestershire sauce. Bring to the boil, then reduce the heat, cover, and simmer for 20 minutes.

3 Meanwhile, to make the dumplings, place the flour in a bowl and stir in the suet, parsley, and dried herbs, and season with salt and pepper. Stir in 5–6 tablespoons of cold water, or just enough to make a soft, not sticky, dough. With lightly floured hands, divide into 12 balls.

4 Remove the casserole lid and arrange the dumplings over the top. Cover and simmer for a further 20 minutes, or until the dumplings are risen and fluffy. Serve in the casserole.

serves 4

prep 15 mins
• cook 50 mins

large flameproof casserole

freeze, without dumplings, for up to 3 months

Coq au vin

A French classic that is perfect for entertaining.

INGREDIENTS

2 tbsp plain flour
salt and freshly ground black pepper
1 large chicken, jointed
60g (2 oz) butter
125g (4½ oz) pancetta,
  cut into thick short strips
2 garlic cloves, crushed
1 carrot, cut into cubes
1 celery stick, roughly chopped
4 tbsp brandy or Cognac

750ml (1¼ pints) red wine,
  such as Burgundy or Beaujolais
1 bay leaf
4–5 sprigs of thyme
1 tbsp olive oil
450g (1lb) button onions
1 tsp brown sugar
1 tsp red wine vinegar
225g (8 oz) small mushrooms

METHOD

1 Season the flour with salt and pepper. Coat the chicken with 1 tablespoon of the seasoned flour. Melt half the butter in the casserole, add the chicken, and fry gently until golden brown on all sides.
2 Add the pancetta, garlic, carrot, and celery, and fry until softened. Add the remaining flour and cook for 1–2 minutes. Pour in the brandy and wine, stirring to remove any sediment from the bottom of the casserole. Add the bay leaf and thyme, bring to the boil, cover, and simmer for 1 hour.
3 Meanwhile, melt the rest of the butter with the olive oil in a frying pan. Add the onions and fry until just brown. Stir in the sugar, vinegar, and 1 tablespoon of water.
4 Add the onions and mushrooms to the chicken, and cook for another 30 minutes, or until the chicken is cooked through and the vegetables are tender.
5 Transfer the chicken and vegetables to a hot serving dish. Discard the bay leaf and thyme. Skim off any excess fat and boil the sauce for 3–5 minutes, or until reduced. Pour over the chicken and serve with mashed potatoes and green vegetables.

serves 4

prep 30 mins
• cook 1 hr
30 mins

large flameproof
casserole

freeze for up
to 3 months

Chicken chow mein

This popular Chinese dish is a colourful, tasty medley of noodles, chicken, mushrooms, and vegetables.

INGREDIENTS

4 tsp vegetable oil

4 spring onions, cut into 2.5cm (1in) lengths

2cm (¾in) piece of fresh root ginger, peeled and grated

140g (5 oz) shiitake mushrooms or oyster mushrooms, sliced

1 red pepper, deseeded and chopped

6 skinless boneless chicken thighs, cut into bite-sized pieces

115g (4 oz) green beans, cut into 2.5cm (1in) lengths

350g (12 oz) fresh fine egg noodles

4 tbsp light soy sauce, plus extra for sprinkling

1 tbsp rice wine or dry sherry

120ml (4fl oz) chicken stock

1 tsp cornflour

METHOD

1 Heat half the oil in a wok or large frying pan and stir-fry the spring onions, ginger, mushrooms, and red pepper over high heat for 5 minutes. Remove and set aside.

2 Add the remaining oil and stir-fry the chicken over a high heat for 3 minutes, in separate batches if necessary, then remove from the pan and set aside.

3 Add the green beans and stir-fry for 2 minutes. Add the noodles and return the chicken and vegetables to the pan.

4 Mix together the soy sauce, rice wine or dry sherry, stock, and cornflour until smooth and well blended, then pour into the pan. Toss everything together for 2 minutes, or until piping hot.

5 Serve immediately, with extra soy sauce to sprinkle over.

serves 4

prep 15 mins • cook 15 mins

wok

Special fried rice

INGREDIENTS

900g (2lb) basmati rice
salt and freshly ground black pepper
5 tbsp sunflower oil
450g (1lb) (shelled weight) uncooked
 shrimps or prawns, peeled,
 deveined, and chopped
4 large skinless chicken fillets, cut into
 2.5cm (1in) strips
425g (15 oz) pancetta, cubed
225g (8 oz) white mushrooms, diced

7.5cm (3in) piece of fresh root ginger,
 peeled and finely sliced
225g (8 oz) frozen peas, defrosted
4 eggs, lightly beaten
2 tbsp dark soy sauce
2 tbsp mirin
1 bunch of spring onions, finely sliced
small handful of flat-leaf parsley, finely
 chopped

METHOD

1 Rinse the rice well, then place in a large pan, cover with boiling water, and add a pinch of salt. Cover with a lid, bring to the boil, and cook for 15–20 minutes, or until done. Drain well and put to one side to cool completely.

2 Meanwhile, heat 1 tablespoon of the oil in a wok over a high heat, add the shrimps or prawns, season with salt and pepper, and cook for 10 minutes, or until pink. Remove with a slotted spoon and put to one side. Heat another tablespoon of the oil in the wok, add the chicken, season with salt and pepper, and stir-fry for 10 minutes, or until no longer pink. Remove with a slotted spoon and put to one side.

3 Heat another tablespoon of the oil in the wok, add the pancetta, and cook over a medium-high heat for 6–8 minutes, or until crispy and golden. Remove with a slotted spoon and put to one side. Wipe the wok out with kitchen paper, then heat another tablespoon of the oil in it. Add the mushrooms and ginger, and stir-fry for 5 minutes, or until the mushrooms start to soften. Add the peas for the last minute or two. Remove with a slotted spoon and put to one side.

4 Heat the remaining oil in the wok, then pour in the eggs and cook gently, stirring them around the pan, for 1 minute. Take care not to overcook them. Add the rice and stir well, then stir in the shrimps or prawns, the chicken, pancetta, mushrooms, and peas. Add the soy sauce and mirin and cook for 5 minutes, stirring all the time. Transfer to a large shallow serving dish, top with the spring onions and parsley, and serve.

serves 8

prep 15 mins,
plus cooling
• cook 40 mins

wok

Navarin of lamb

This classic French stew is traditionally made with young spring vegetables.

INGREDIENTS

15g (½ oz) butter

1 tbsp olive oil

900g (2lb) middle neck of lamb, cut into pieces

2 small onions, quartered

1 tbsp plain flour

400ml (14fl oz) lamb stock or beef stock

2 tbsp tomato purée

1 bouquet garni

salt and freshly ground black pepper

300g (10 oz) small new potatoes

300g (10 oz) small whole carrots

300g (10 oz) baby turnips

175g (6 oz) French beans

METHOD

1 Melt the butter with the oil in a large flameproof casserole, add the lamb, and fry until brown on all sides. Add the onions and fry gently for 5 minutes, stirring frequently.

2 Sprinkle the flour over the meat and stir well for 2 minutes, or until the pieces are evenly coated. Stir in the stock, then add the tomato purée and bouquet garni, and season to taste with salt and pepper. Bring to the boil, then cover and simmer for 45 minutes.

3 Add the potatoes, carrots, and turnips. Cover and cook for a further 15 minutes, then stir in the beans, cover, and cook for a further 10–15 minutes, or until all the vegetables are tender.

serves 4

prep 30 mins
• cook 1 hr
30 mins

large flameproof
casserole

freeze for up
to 3 months

Irish stew

Made with lamb and potatoes, this dish is slow-cooked for maximum flavour and tenderness.

INGREDIENTS

8 best-end neck of lamb chops,
  about 750g (1lb 10 oz) total weight
800g (1¾lb) onions, sliced
3 carrots, thickly sliced
800g (1¾lb) floury potatoes,
  peeled and thickly sliced
salt and freshly ground black pepper
large sprig of thyme
1 bay leaf
600ml (1 pint) lamb stock or beef stock

METHOD

1 Preheat the oven to 160°C (325°F/Gas 3).
2 Layer the lamb, onions, carrots, and one-third of the potato slices in a large, heavy casserole. Season with salt and pepper between the layers.
3 Tuck the thyme and bay leaf into the ingredients, then top with the remaining potato slices. Pour the stock over, cover, and place in the oven for 1 hour.
4 Remove the lid and return the casserole to the oven for a further 30–40 minutes, or until the top is browned. Serve hot, with a fresh green vegetable, such as spring greens, kale, or broccoli.

serves 4–6

prep 20 mins
• cook 1 hr 40 mins

Lamb tagine with couscous

The dried apricots, cumin, coriander, ginger, and thyme that flavour this dish are typical of Moroccan cuisine.

INGREDIENTS

1 onion, thinly sliced
1 tsp ground coriander
1 tsp ground cumin
1 tsp ground ginger
1 tsp dried thyme
2 tbsp sunflower oil or peanut oil
900g (2lb) boneless lamb, such as
   shoulder or chump steaks, cut into
   2.5cm (1in) cubes

2 tbsp plain flour
300ml (10fl oz) orange juice
600ml (1 pint) chicken stock
115g (4 oz) no-soak dried apricots
salt and freshly ground black pepper
mint leaves, to garnish
200g (7 oz) quick-cook couscous
salt

METHOD

1 Put the onion, coriander, cumin, ginger, thyme, and 1 tablespoon of the oil in a large, non-metallic bowl, then mix in the lamb. Cover and refrigerate for at least 3 hours or overnight to marinate.

2 When ready to cook, preheat the oven to 160°C (325°F/Gas 3). Put the flour in a small bowl and slowly stir in the orange juice until smooth, then set aside.

3 Heat the remaining oil in a large, flameproof casserole over a high heat. Add the lamb mixture and fry, stirring frequently, for 5 minutes, or until browned.

4 Stir the orange juice mixture into the casserole with the stock. Bring to the boil, stirring, then remove the casserole from the heat, cover, and place in the oven for 1 hour.

5 Remove the casserole from the oven. Stir in the apricots, cover and return to the oven. Cook for a further 20 minutes, or until the lamb is tender.

6 Meanwhile, put the couscous with a pinch of salt in a large heatproof bowl and pour over 2.5cm (1in) of boiling water. Cover with a folded tea towel and leave to stand for 10 minutes, or until the grains are tender. Fluff with a fork and keep warm. When the lamb is tender, taste and adjust the seasoning. Sprinkle with mint leaves and serve the lamb with the hot couscous.

serves 4

prep 10 mins, plus marinating • cook 1 hr 30 mins

marinate for at least 3 hrs

large flameproof casserole

freeze for up to 1 month

Hungarian goulash

This warming winter stew makes a great main course if you are entertaining, as all the hard work can be done in advance.

INGREDIENTS

4 tbsp oil

900g (2lb) braising steak, cut into
  2.5cm (1in) cubes

2 large onions, thinly sliced

2 garlic cloves, crushed

2 red peppers, deseeded and chopped

1 tbsp paprika, plus extra to garnish

400g can chopped tomatoes

2 tbsp tomato purée

1 tbsp plain flour

300ml (10fl oz) beef stock

1 tsp chopped thyme

salt and freshly ground black pepper

150ml (5fl oz) soured cream

METHOD

1 Preheat the oven to 160°C (325°F/Gas 3).

2 Heat half the oil in a large frying pan and brown the meat in batches, transferring to a large casserole as they finish browning.

3 Add the remaining oil to the pan, lower the heat, and fry the onions, garlic, and peppers until soft. Stir in the paprika and cook for 1 minute, then add the tomatoes and tomato purée. Mix the flour with a little stock until smooth, then pour it into the pan with the rest of the stock. Bring to the boil, stirring often. Add the thyme, season to taste with salt and pepper, then pour the sauce into the casserole.

4 Cover tightly and place in the oven for 2 hours, or until the beef is very tender.

5 To serve, spoon the goulash into individual bowls and top each serving with a couple of spoonfuls of soured cream and sprinkle with a little paprika. Goulash is delicious served with buttered tagliatelle.

serves 4

prep 25 mins
• cook 2 hrs
30 mins

freeze, without the
soured cream, for
up to 3 months

Pork and bean stew

INGREDIENTS

500g (1lb 2oz) dried black-eyed beans
2 pig's trotters
250g (9 oz) smoked pork ribs
175g (6 oz) smoked streaky bacon,
  left in 1 piece
200g can chopped tomatoes
1 tbsp tomato purée
1 bay leaf
salt and freshly ground black pepper

oil, for frying
500g (1lb 2oz) lean pork fillet or steaks
1 small onion, finely chopped
2 garlic cloves, finely chopped
175g (6 oz) chorizo sausage, cut into
  small chunks
1 green chilli, deseeded (optional)
1 orange, cut into wedges, to garnish
3 spring onions, chopped, to garnish

METHOD

1 Rinse the beans, place in a bowl, and pour over cold water to cover. Leave overnight.

2 Drain the beans and place in a large saucepan. Cover with fresh water, bring to the boil, and boil for 10 minutes, skimming off any scum, then lower the heat, cover and simmer for 1 hour.

3 Meanwhile, place the pig's trotters, pork ribs, and streaky bacon in a saucepan with the canned tomatoes and their juice, the tomato purée, bay leaf, and salt and pepper to taste. Add enough cold water to cover, bring to the boil, skim off any scum, cover, reduce the heat and simmer for 50 minutes.

4 Drain the beans and reserve the cooking liquid, then return the beans to the pan. Add the meats with their cooking liquid. Add just enough of the reserved cooking liquid from the beans to cover. Continue to cook, covered, over a low heat, for another 20 minutes.

5 Heat 1 tablespoon of oil in a frying pan and brown the pork fillet. Add to the meat and bean mixture and continue to cook for a further 10 minutes, or until the meat is tender and the beans very soft. Wipe out the frying pan, add 1 tablespoon of oil and fry the onion and garlic over medium heat for 3–4 minutes, stirring frequently, until soft and translucent. Add the chorizo and chilli, if using, and fry for a further 2 minutes, stirring. Add 2–3 tablespoons of the cooked beans to the frying pan and mash well with the back of a spoon. Add the contents of the frying pan to the meat and beans, stir, and cook for a further 10 minutes.

6 To serve, remove the larger pieces of meat and cut into smaller pieces. Transfer them and the rest of the meat and bean mixture on to a serving dish and garnish with orange wedges and spring onions. Serve immediately.

serves 6–8

prep 1 hr 15 mins,
plus soaking
• cook 1 hr 35 mins

the beans need
to be soaked
the day before

Chicken with broad beans

This easy recipe is also versatile: try it with good-quality sausages for a variation.

INGREDIENTS

8 chicken thighs
salt and freshly ground black pepper
2 tbsp olive oil
1 onion, finely chopped
2 celery sticks, finely chopped
2 garlic cloves, grated or finely chopped

a few sprigs of rosemary, leaves picked and finely chopped
1 large glass of dry white wine
200g (7 oz) frozen broad beans, or fresh if in season
500ml (16fl oz) hot chicken stock

METHOD

1 Preheat the oven to 200°C (400°F/Gas 6). Season the chicken pieces well with salt and black pepper. Heat 1 tablespoon of the oil in a large flameproof casserole over a medium-high heat. Add the chicken, skin-side down, and brown for 5–6 minutes on each side until golden all over. Remove from the pan, and set aside.

2 Reduce the heat to low, and add the remaining oil to the casserole. Add the onion and a pinch of salt, and sweat for 5 minutes until soft. Now add the celery, garlic, and rosemary, and sweat for a further 5 minutes. Increase the heat, pour in the wine, and let simmer for about 5 minutes.

3 Stir through the broad beans, and return the chicken to the pan, tucking the pieces in and around the beans. Pour the stock over, cover, and cook in the oven for 45 minutes to 1 hour. Check halfway through the cooking time, topping up with a little hot water if too dry. Serve with oven-roasted tomatoes and fresh crusty bread.

serves 4

prep 10 mins
• cook 1 hr

large flameproof casserole

Burgundy beef

In this classic French casserole, *Boeuf Bourguignon*, long, slow braising ensures the meat becomes tender.

INGREDIENTS

175g (6 oz) streaky bacon rashers, chopped
1–2 tbsp oil
900g (2lb) braising steak, cut into 4cm (1½in) cubes
12 small shallots
1 tbsp plain flour
300ml (10fl oz) red wine

300ml (10fl oz) beef stock
115g (4 oz) button mushrooms
1 bay leaf
1 tsp dried herbes de Provence
salt and freshly ground black pepper
4 tbsp flat-leaf parsley, chopped
mashed potatoes, to serve

METHOD

1 Preheat the oven to 160°C (325°F/Gas 3). Fry the bacon in a non-stick frying pan until lightly browned. Drain on kitchen paper and transfer to a casserole.

2 Depending on how much fat is left from the bacon, add a little oil to the pan if necessary so that you have about 2–3 tablespoons. Fry the beef in batches over a high heat, transferring to the casserole as they brown.

3 Reduce the heat to medium and fry the shallots. Transfer to the casserole and stir the flour into the remaining fat in the frying pan. If the pan is quite dry, mix the flour with a little of the wine or stock. Pour the wine and stock into the frying pan and bring to the boil, stirring constantly until smooth.

4 Add the mushrooms, bay leaf, and dried herbs. Season to taste with salt and pepper and pour the contents of the pan over the meat and shallots in the casserole. Cover and cook in the oven for 2 hours, or until the meat is very tender.

5 Sprinkle with chopped parsley and serve hot with mashed potatoes.

serves 4

prep 25 mins
• cook 2 hrs 30 mins

freeze for up to 3 months

Sweet potato and butterbean stew

A satisfying vegetarian supper dish that is heavenly on winter evenings.

INGREDIENTS

450g (1lb) sweet potatoes,
    peeled and cut into thick slices
2 tbsp maple syrup
1 tbsp olive oil
1 red onion, finely chopped
1 tsp cumin seeds
salt and freshly ground black pepper

400g can peeled whole plum
    tomatoes, chopped
splash of balsamic vinegar
400g can butterbeans, drained and rinsed
handful of Swiss chard or spinach leaves
150ml (5fl oz) Greek-style yogurt
handful of mint leaves, to garnish

METHOD

1 Cook the sweet potatoes and maple syrup in a large wide pan of boiling salted water for 10 minutes until tender, but not too soft. Drain well, set aside, and keep warm.

2 Meanwhile, heat the oil in a large wide pan or deep frying pan over a low heat. Add the onion, cumin seeds, and a pinch of salt, and sweat for about 5 minutes until the onion is soft and translucent. Tip in the tomatoes, including any juices, and the balsamic vinegar, and cook for about 10 minutes. Taste, and season with salt and pepper.

3 Add the butterbeans, and simmer for a further 5 minutes, then stir through the Swiss chard or spinach. Cook for a couple of minutes more until the leaves just wilt. Remove from the heat, and top with the sweet potatoes. Preheat the grill to hot.

4 Transfer to an ovenproof dish, top with yogurt, and grill until golden. Garnish with mint leaves.

serves 4

prep 10 mins
• cook 30 mins

Daube of beef with wild mushrooms

This rich stew benefits from being made a few days before serving so the flavours can develop.

INGREDIENTS

2 tbsp olive oil

30g (1 oz) butter

900g (2lb) chuck steak, cut into 7.5cm (3in) pieces

2 tbsp plain flour

salt and freshly ground black pepper

115g (4 oz) rindless bacon rashers, chopped

2 small onions, finely chopped

3 garlic cloves, crushed

1 celery stick, finely chopped

3 carrots, diced

1 tbsp chopped fresh or dried thyme

900ml (1½ pints) red wine

2 tbsp brandy (optional)

zest and juice of 1 orange

175g (6 oz) field mushrooms

30g (1 oz) dried mushrooms

1 tbsp tomato purée

METHOD

1 Heat the olive oil and butter in the casserole. Coat the meat in seasoned flour, then brown on all sides in the casserole. Remove the pieces to a warm plate.

2 Fry the bacon, onions, garlic, and celery in the casserole, until lightly coloured. Stir in the beef along with the carrots and thyme. Pour in the red wine, the brandy, and the orange zest and juice; bring to the boil, stirring, then reduce the heat, cover, and simmer for 1 hour.

3 Meanwhile, clean and slice the field mushrooms. Put the dried mushrooms in a bowl and pour over boiling water. Leave to soak for 15 minutes, then drain, dry, and chop. Stir the mushrooms and the tomato purée into the casserole.

4 Cover and continue to simmer for another 30 minutes, or until the meat is very tender. Serve while still hot with boiled potatoes, fried bread triangles, and a sprinkling of chopped flat-leaf parsley.

serves 6

prep 30 mins
• cook 2 hrs

flameproof casserole with a tight-fitting lid

freeze for up to 3 months

Rosemary and chilli sausages with new potatoes

This roast is flavourful and extremely easy to do – it's ideal for lazy Sundays.

INGREDIENTS

8–12 good-quality pork sausages
2 red onions, peeled and cut
   into eighths
pinch of chilli flakes
handful of rosemary stalks
1.1kg (2½lb) new potatoes,
   large ones halved
salt and freshly ground
   black pepper
1 tbsp olive oil

METHOD

1 Preheat the oven to 200°C (400°F/Gas 6). Put the sausages in a roasting tin along with the onion, sprinkle over the chilli flakes and rosemary, then add the new potatoes. Season well with salt and pepper, then drizzle over the oil and combine everything together well.

2 Put in the oven to roast for 30–40 minutes, or until the sausages are golden all over and cooked through. Turn the sausages and potatoes halfway through cooking.

serves 4

prep 15 mins
• cook 40 mins

Arroz con pollo

This is a colourful chicken and rice dish from Latin America.

INGREDIENTS

2 tbsp olive oil
8 chicken thighs
1 Spanish onion, finely sliced
1 green pepper, deseeded and chopped
1 red pepper, deseeded and chopped
2 garlic cloves, finely chopped
1 tsp smoked paprika
1 bay leaf
230g can chopped tomatoes

1 tsp thyme leaves
1 tsp dried oregano
175g (6 oz) long-grain rice
pinch of saffron threads
750ml (1¼ pints) chicken stock
2 tbsp tomato purée
juice of ½ lemon
salt and freshly ground black pepper
100g (3½ oz) frozen peas

METHOD

1 Preheat the oven to 180°C (350°F/Gas 4). Heat half the oil in a large flameproof casserole and fry the chicken thighs over high heat, turning frequently, or until evenly browned. Remove from the casserole, drain on kitchen paper, and set aside.

2 Add the remaining oil, reduce the heat, and fry the onion until softened. Add the chopped peppers and garlic and fry for 5 minutes, or until they start to soften. Add the paprika, bay leaf, chopped tomatoes, thyme, and oregano, and stir in the rice. Fry for 1–2 minutes, stirring constantly.

3 Crumble in the saffron, add the stock, tomato purée, and lemon juice, and season to taste with salt and pepper.

4 Return the chicken thighs to the casserole, pushing them down into the rice, cover, and cook in the oven for 15 minutes. Remove the casserole from the oven, add the peas and return to the oven for a further 10 minutes, or until the rice is tender and has absorbed the cooking liquid. Serve hot, straight from the casserole.

serves 4

prep 20 mins
• cook 45 mins

large flameproof casserole

Pork with rice and tomatoes

Big, bold, and filling – this makes a super family meal.

INGREDIENTS

6 tbsp olive oil
3 onions, diced
1.1kg (2½lb) lean pork, cut into
  5cm (2in) chunks
6 garlic cloves, grated or finely chopped
handful of flat-leaf parsley, chopped
1 tbsp thyme leaves
1 tbsp chopped sage leaves
2 tsp paprika
150ml (5fl oz) dry white wine
550g (1¼lb) long-grain rice
4 x 400g cans chopped tomatoes
salt and freshly ground black pepper

METHOD

1 Preheat the oven to 150°C (300°F/Gas 2). Heat the oil in a large heavy-based pan, add the onions, and cook over a medium heat for 5 minutes, or until starting to soften. Add the pork and cook, stirring occasionally, for 5 minutes, or until no longer pink. Add the garlic, parsley, thyme, sage, and paprika and combine well, then add the wine and cook for 5 minutes. Add the rice and tomatoes, stir to combine, then season well with salt and pepper.

2 Cover with a lid and cook in the oven for 1 hour. Stir occasionally and add a little hot water if it starts to dry out. Remove from the oven and allow to stand for 10 minutes with the lid on before serving.

serves 6–8

prep 30 mins
• cook 1 hr

London, New York, Melbourne, Munich, and Delhi

Senior Editor Cécile Landau

Editorial Assistant Shashwati Tia Sarkar

Designer Elma Aquino

Jacket Designer Mark Penfound

DTP Designer Kavita Varma

DK INDIA

Editorial Consultant Dipali Singh

Designer Neha Ahuja

DTP Designer Tarun Sharma

DTP Coordinator Sunil Sharma

Head of Publishing Aparna Sharma

This edition published in 2013
First published in Great Britain in 2012
Material in this publication was previously published
in *The Cooking Book* (2008) and *Cook Express* (2009)
by Dorling Kindersley Limited
80 Strand, London WC2R 0RL
Penguin Group (UK)

Copyright © 2008, 2009, 2012, 2013 Dorling Kindersley
Text copyright © 2008, 2009, 2012 Dorling Kindersley

10 9 8 7 6 5 4 3 2 1
001–192526–Feb/13

A CIP catalogue record for this book is available
from the British Library.

ISBN 978-1-4093-2591-8

Printed and bound in China by Hung Hing Printing Co. Ltd.